Laura E. Richards

Love and Rocks

Laura E. Richards

Love and Rocks

ISBN/EAN: 9783743306011

Manufactured in Europe, USA, Canada, Australia, Japa

Cover: Foto ©ninafisch / pixelio.de

Manufactured and distributed by brebook publishing software (www.brebook.com)

Laura E. Richards

Love and Rocks

LOVE AND ROCKS

BY
LAURA E. RICHARDS
AUTHOR OF "CAPTAIN JANUARY," "MELODY,"
"FIVE-MINUTE STORIES," ETC.

BOSTON
ESTES AND LAURIAT
MDCCCXCVIII

Copyright, 1898,
BY ESTES AND LAURIAT.

Colonial Press:
Electrotyped and Printed by C. H. Simonds & Co.
Boston, Mass., U. S. A.

TO

James and Mary Barstow

THIS STORY IS AFFECTIONATELY
DEDICATED.

CONTENTS.

CHAPTER		PAGE
I.	Menonquit	11
II.	"All We Like Sheep—"	25
III.	On the Beach	35
IV.	The Black Woods	51
V.	Souvent Femme Varie	67
VI.	The Rock House	80
VII.	"Que les Beaux Jours Sont Courts".	98

LOVE AND ROCKS.

CHAPTER I.

MENONQUIT.

A SQUARE, gray house, substantial and roomy, perched on a crag; the front windows looking down on the white, rock-framed beach, the harbour, and the black mass of Toluma Island opposite; while the back windows command the village street, and the gray fish-houses, with their pleasant confusion of lobster-pots and ropes and boats. This house is the Influence, the oldest house on Menonquit Island, formerly the home of many a stately sea-king, of the early fishers and mariners of Menonquit, now owned and kept by Mrs. Treherne, the bright-eyed and cheery descendant of those kings. This is Mrs. Treherne, standing on the verandah this bright June morning, and the young person beside her is Miss Mary Weymouth, who has come to spend a month on the island of her love. She is looking very cross, which is a pity for so pretty and agreeable a girl. She has seen in the narrow entry of the inn a strange trunk standing beside her own, and her soul is filled with bitterness.

"Oh, Mrs. Treherne! You wrote me that no one else was here. You know I told you that I wished positively to be alone if I came."

"And no one else was here, Miss Weymouth!" responded the landlady, promptly. "I wrote you the truth, and I expected no one till the end of the month; but this young gentleman came here all by himself last night. He was with friends on board a yacht, and got them to leave him here. He wants to be alone, too, and desires nothing but quiet. Real pleasant, he seems! his name is — "

"Oh, never mind his name, Mrs. Treherne! I dare say we shall not interfere with each other. I suppose I can have my meals alone, can I? And did you remember the room I liked so much last year?"

"Yes, indeed!" said Mrs. Treherne. "It is all ready for you; and, as for meals, the gentleman was particular about having his meals an hour before every one else, and he expects to live outdoors most of the time. I dare say you won't set eyes on each other from one day to another."

"I dare say not!" said Miss Weymouth. "But it is exasperating, all the same!" she said to herself, when she was left alone in her own room, the corner room that looked out over the great south down and the sea beyond it.

"I did think I could find solitude on Menonquit in June. Why could not this stupid person have been left on Matinicus, or at Christmas Cove, or Owl's Head, or anywhere else but here?

"There he is now!" and she drew back from the window, taking refuge behind the muslin curtain.

"Harvard, if ever I saw it! Humph! Yes, not a doubt of it. John Harvard, sir, is what I shall call you, since luckily I did not hear your other name. Oh, you tiresome creature!" She shook her head and retired, as the young man came up the steps of the Influence. He was a stalwart, broad-shouldered fellow, who walked lightly enough, yet set his feet down with weight and purpose. There may have been a slight Harvard swing to his arms, though people can swing their arms elsewhere, it has been asserted.

He came into the hall, whistling "Toreador," his brown eyes shining, his face alight with cheerfulness; but came to a dead stop before the two trunks in the entry. His face fell.

"Oh, I say!" he murmured. "I didn't

bargain for this, you know. They told me there wasn't a soul on the island except the people themselves."

He surveyed the peaceful trunk with profound disgust, which deepened as he read the legend upon it.

"M. W., Smith College."

"I ask you, is a person called upon to endure this? I wonder at you, Miss Smith; yes, I do! Miss Smith you shall be to me. You probably dislike the name, and anything to give pain, as Michael Finsbury says. But to think of my not letting Tom come ashore with me, because I wanted to try it alone, and do a lot of thinking, — and then having to foregather with Smith College. My dear miss, you must not expect it!" And muttering unseemly remarks concerning educational establishments for women, this young gentleman went in to his supper.

Next morning the trunks were gone from the entry, and the young man, coming out on the verandah for his after-breakfast smoke, had almost forgotten the newcomer, till he caught a glimpse of a slight figure in a short blue skirt and jacket, with two long braids of hair hanging down, and a Tam-o'-Shanter cap atop. The girl's face was turned towards him for an instant only, but he saw that it was rosy and youthful, with a pair of wide-open blue eyes, and a determined little mouth. He gave an inward whistle as she disappeared. "Sixteen, and pretty! I looked for twenty-eight, and spectacled. A forward chit, indeed, to be frisking it alone on islands; but so the century closes! And, after all, there is no one for her to run away with, if she were so minded."

He tramped up and down the verandah, smoking cheerfully, trying to whistle at the same time, and making elaborate plans for an all-day sketching tramp.

Mary Weymouth, waiting at the corner for a chance to slip by unseen and get away, regarded him with unfriendly eyes.

"Oh, you stupid! Why can't you smoke your horrid pipe somewhere else? Blocking up the way like this! I wish they had a chair of sense at Harvard! It's disgraceful!"

Finally, out of all patience, she waited till the stranger turned his back, and then fairly ran across the verandah; and, as the young man turned again, he saw her light figure, black against the glowing sky, flitting over the hill.

"Exeunt pigtails!" he said. "The child avoids me; 'tis well!" and he waved his pipe in salutation. "Be good, sweet maid, and continue to shun my baleful presence—

'Flower o' the peach!
Death for us all, and his own life for each!'

And after all, one small girl is not so much matter on an island three miles long."

Mary Weymouth, never looking back, took her way down towards the south rocks. "Just for ten minutes!" she said to herself. "Just ten minutes' conversation with the shrimps and crabs, — then the yew-hollow, and reflection!"

The island lay green and fair under the June sun, ringed with its black rocks, which struck sharply against the tossing blue of the sea. In the harbour, — if so one may call the narrow gut which lies between the island and its sister, Toluma, — the water was smoother than outside, and here the fishers were busy in their boats, hoisting sail and standing out to sea; some of them were already out and away, and their sails shone in the sun like patches of gleaming snow.

Mary Weymouth stepped from rock to rock, now singing bits of sea-song, now talking to herself. She was happy. All winter she had longed for the island. She had seen it last year for the first time, though its name had been familiar all her life; her people had come from here, — started from here to California, far back in the forties. And when she came, in those first homesick weeks before the college term began, and with it the new, strange life, — lo, it was a home to which she came.

All the stories that her grandmother had told her, all the wild pictures her child-mind had formed of the lonely island, sea-beaten and wind-swept, which her grandfather left because he did not love the fishing —

("But his heart stayed there, my dear!" said Grandmother Weymouth. "His heart stayed there, and he longed for it all his life.") —

These things had made the black rocks, and the free hilltops, and the deep-bosomed valleys, welcome her as their own child. She felt that it was all her own, her birthright, her heritage.

The island people were her friends by inheritance; she would make them so by love, give her only a little time alone with them. But for the strangers, the summer visitors, the artists, and the rare excursionists, Mary felt a fierce scorn. She called it hatred, but she was only twenty. She had passed them with head held high, and eyes that saw nothing. What business had they here, on her island? They had no graves in the gray enclosure on the lighthouse hill. No voices called to them from cliff and wood and vale. Why could they not go to the Isles of Shoals, or anywhere else, and leave her alone with her own?

So when this summer came, with its great question to decide, she had flown like a bird to her mountain, the very hour college closed, feeling sure that now she should have her island all to herself, and could wander and think at her ease.

Well, — and after all, — of course it was annoying, but how was one young Harvard sprig to interfere with her? Now that the matter of the meals was settled, and there was no actual need of their ever coming in contact, she could forget him, or consider him in the light of a post.

The rocks gleamed black and wet where the tide had gone down. The little pools were gay with green and crimson mosses, and alive with all manner of cheerful inhabitants; below, the foam came curling up, caressing, inviting. How pleasant it would be to sit and dip one's feet —

"No!" said Mary, with decision. "No! I am going to the yew-hollow. I said I would reflect, and I will; and it would not be possible here, with everything making eyes at me like this."

She struck upward over the down that heaved its great shoulder towards the south end of the island. By and by she came to a little dell that lay open to the sun, with the sea looking in at one end. The bottom was a plot of russet grass, with water twinkling wherever a sunbeam struck; the sloping sides were covered with a dense mat of trailing yew. Mary threw herself down on the elastic bed, and inhaled its fragrance with deep breaths.

"Oh, good! Oh, native!" she cried. "I was born here, one of me. Just smell it, will you? And taste!" she added, plucking one of the gray-blue berries, and crushing it between her teeth.

"Talk of the almond and rose of Damascus! H'm! Let them come here! No! Let them stay away, I mean. And now, let me think!"

The question of a career! What should she do with her life? It lay before her, as the sea lay here; these gates of green, with the blue shining beyond them, were the gates of womanhood opening before her. Yes! she must decide now, and shape the three years of college yet remaining to fit the future towards which she looked. That was why she had come here to the island; to be alone, to think and to plan. Yes!

How blue the sea! Was that the mail

schooner, just in sight? The Captain ought to have had a great "chance," such a morning as this.

Literature! There was a field! One of the greatest in the world. And talking of fields, that green knoll where she had seen the sheep huddled together this morning would be a lovely place to sit in!

Literature!— or medicine! Only one didn't like drugs, and they were finding out such horrible things every day. One could no longer enjoy the privacy of one's own bones. And talking of drugs, was there any drug or spice so sweet as this yew? Could not some wonderful balsam be made from it that should cure all diseases, nerves and things? "And there came no more any such spices as the Queen of Sheba brought to King Solomon." This might be Balsam of Sheba, or Solomon's Strength, or — anything — alliterative.

The sun beat down on the yew bed, and fresh puffs of warm perfume crept from it. The scent was going to her head! Perfumes used to poison,— did they intoxicate first? The sun was very warm — literature — a great field — full of brown grass — and yew —

Silence! The sea lapping on the crags below. The girl asleep under the summer blue, white gulls wheeling above, white clouds floating,— silence!

"Literature!" said Mary again, sitting up straight and looking about her wide-eyed.

A new fragrance was in her nostrils; a faint blue smoke hung near her in curling, fading rings; was it — could it be — tobacco smoke?

And just beyond the seaward end of the dell, a loose stone rolled from under a hasty foot, and went dropping down from ledge to ledge till it plunged in the water. Then silence again.

"Impertinence!" said Mary Weymouth.

CHAPTER II.

"ALL WE LIKE SHEEP —"

IT is difficult to do much deep thinking when one is exploring the country of one's heart. Mary Weymouth started out every morning with her heart full of courage and her head full of ideas; she came back at night rosy, happy-eyed, unconscious of anything save the sea and the rocks, the rocks and the sea.

To-day, for example, she was determined to consider the subject of education as a profession. Learning should be her comrade, and she would think from morning till night of a teacher's life; put herself into it as into a frame, and look at herself. After all, what could be more useful than teaching, and for what could she so well fit herself?

Starting out, she met the children of the village on their way to school; and full of pleasure and friendly impulse, she stopped to exchange greetings with them. Some of the children replied cheerfully, others hung their heads and put fingers in their mouths, while others still fairly ran away when she asked how they liked their school and what were their favourite lessons.

She would change all that, if she taught children; and she shook her head gravely as she climbed the hill. Her pupils should learn from the first to be gracious, courteous to strangers, full of smiles and cordiality. Perhaps she might better begin the day by going to the school, talking with the teacher, perhaps suggesting to her these ideas. No! On the whole, the afternoon would do as well, and it would be wicked to spend such a morning as this within four walls.

Graciousness! It was a duty that every one owed to his fellow beings — here the

"ALL WE LIKE SHEEP—" 27

young lady looked up, and saw coming towards her the fellow being who was also her fellow lodger; and she turned off into the field, and almost ran up the hillside, over the brow, into the hollow beyond.

Seated on a comfortable boulder, she reflected, and became aware of inconsistency in her behaviour. Graciousness! It was a duty that every one owed —

"Oh! I can't help it!" she said, shrugging her shoulders. "I must be allowed to live!" and then she looked about her, and the place possessed her.

The rocks ran in long, gray ridges, climbing up here and there into pinnacles and cairns. Between the ridges the grass was green as emerald, and water trickled everywhere in silent rills, or stood in pools to catch the sky. Wherever the green was broken, the soil showed black and rich like peat.

Old, twisted firs stood here and there, like crabbed green dwarfs, guarding the fairy hollows. "I was born *here!*" cried

Mary, spreading her arms wide to clasp the brightness and the beauty of it. Then she stepped along from tuft to tuft of long grass, feeling the water pleasantly cool through her canvas shoes. Presently she came to where a granite ridge had been rent apart, and formed a gateway; she passed through this, and found herself in a pretty place indeed.

The gray rocks shut in a space some twenty feet across either way; the grass was firm and short and green, — how green! That was all, — grass and granite, and a sky burning blue overhead; but the rocks huddled together in all possible shapes, quaint or solemn, and here and there were clefts between them, running back into blackness, suggestive of all manner of delightful mystery.

One such cleft invited Mary to explore it. The entrance was low, and she must creep in on hands and knees; but once inside she could sit upright, and fancy herself a fair anchorite in a cell of the

Thebaid, studying the question of education.

"It smells a little sheepy," she said, "and it might be convenient to stand up or turn round once in a while, — say every seven years or so, — but on the whole an enchanting place! I can certainly meditate here, for there is nothing to capture the eyes, — only good, solid stone wall, and the peep of blue and green outside. Now I will think about education in good earnest. Gracious! What is that?"

She listened and looked, and looking, felt her blood turn slowly to ice.

Into the little rock-parlour from which she had just retreated stepped an active figure that Mary already knew too well. Pipe in mouth, sketching tools in hand, — humming "Toreador" through his teeth, — John Harvard came! Oh, distraction! oh, horror! the hateful, odious man! he was sitting down, — he was opening his sketch-book, — he was actually establishing himself for the morning!

Seated with his back turned squarely to the cave, facing the entrance of the rock-parlour, the young man drew a deep breath of satisfaction, and addressed the universe. "Comfortable? Yes, thank you! I do believe this the prettiest bit I have found yet. No vile humanity to disturb the fantastic pannicles!" And he fell to sketching, with ardour, the entrancing view framed by the stony gates; the black fir that leaned across, the shimmering foreground, the living blue beyond.

What was to be done? The ice in Mary's veins melted, glowed, turned to liquid fire. If she could only rush out, with a shriek that should paralyse him, should prevent him from turning round; rush out, and past him, and away! But there was to be no rushing. She had crept in forwards, she must creep out backwards, on her hands and knees. Well, she would not do that! She would sooner die in the cave!

This being settled, Miss Weymouth

became aware of cramps in her foot; she was sitting with it doubled up under her, for there was not room to stretch both feet out. She remembered reading how an actress, — Miss Cushman, was it? — to help her sister, smitten with stage-fright, crouched motionless in one position for half an hour. Oh, well, but if you came to that, there were the Indian fakirs, who held their arms up straight till they stiffened. Oh! — oh! but Mary was not a fakir. Slowly and cautiously she drew her foot out; it struck a pebble, and sent it rattling to the entrance. She held her breath; but the sketcher took no notice.

"To — *re* — ador!" he sang abstractedly, mixing shades of blue, with one eye on the horizon. Mary noticed that he had a delightful voice, and hated him the more for it.

"Oh, you goose! why can't you go *out* of the door?" she muttered under her breath.

It was her back now; the rock was sticking into it, hard and knobby. The smell of sheep grew stronger. Oh! why, why had she ever got into this dreadful little hole? She *could* not stay here all the morning; she should die!

How long had she been here now? It seemed hours. If she could only sleep! She shut her eyes, and repeated Shelley's "Hymn to Night," as she had been advised to do when her nerves required soothing. Then she parodied it:

> "Swiftly walk *into* the western wave,
> Hideous fright!
> Off from the entrance of this cave,
> Where all the long and lone daylight
> Thou keepest me a prisoner here,
> In sheepy dungeon, dark and drear, —
> Swift be thy flight."

But sleep did not come, and the aches grew and multiplied; and at length it came over Mary that she could not bear the situation any longer. She must come out; she did not care what happened.

Softly, slowly she began to move backward towards the mouth of the cavern. If she could only get out, get upright on her feet before he turned round! Vain hope! Another pebble rattled and rolled, — another!

"Hallo!" said John Harvard. He turned, and his bright, dark eyes looked directly into the cave.

"Something in there! Sheep! Come out, sheep! Come out, I say!" He was looking about for a stone to throw, with a view to dislodging the intruder, when a voice came from the depths, icy and tremulous:

"Do not — throw stones! I — am coming out!"

The voice broke off suddenly; the young man did not hear the sob, but he felt it. He sprang to his feet and pulled off his cap, keeping his back carefully turned to the cave.

"I *beg* your pardon!" he said. "I'm awfully sorry! You — you are sure you don't need any help?"

Mary tried to say, "No, thank you!" but the words would not come out straight. She crept out, the pebbles rolling to right and left, scrambled to her feet and turned to flee; but in the rocky gateway she paused. Her breath was coming painfully short and quick, but she pulled herself together, and said, with tolerable distinctness, "I thank you, — sir, — for your considerateness."

"May I turn round now?" asked John Harvard, meekly.

"Oh, of course you may!" cried Mary, angrily. "Good-morning!"

He turned quickly, but not quickly enough; the last fold of a blue skirt fluttered and vanished. Hasty feet fled away over the down towards the shore.

"Miss Smith," said John Harvard, "*I* call that a scurvy trick!"

CHAPTER III.

ON THE BEACH.

FOR some time after this Mary lived in peace. She had no further trouble from her fellow lodger. Perhaps he was exploring the further end of the island; at all events, he came no more to her favourite haunts. Only in the evening she would hear his springing step and his cheery whistle, as he came running up the steps and passed through the narrow entry on his way to the dining-room. He never so much as looked in at the parlour door; and being thus safe from annoyance, Mary gradually got into the way of listening for the whistle and the light, firm tread. He was a punctual creature, she acknowledged; really almost as good as a clock. One night, it is true, she was very angry, because he stood under her window and sang for an hour. It was full moon; he stood by the verandah rail, and certainly he was very good-looking, — and graceful, — and his voice was enchanting. Still, it was impertinent; not that she really supposed he was audacious enough to fancy that she was listening to him, but still, — even the proximity to her window, and the absence of any one but herself to whom he could sing, — in short, it was an impertinence, and Mary was furious. She did not go to bed very early, — it was full moon, as I said, and the glory of it unspeakable; and when she did, all was silent except the sea, and the last song was ringing in her ears. It had a quaint little refrain, evidently a song of Stuart times, Mary thought. She was rather well up in Stuart songs; she had taken a course in them this very year.

"Oh, it's never yet the blade I met
  Could prick to bring me pain.
Oh, it's never yet the maid I met
  I sighed to meet again.
Then it's hey! for a horse!
A hound and a horse!
And over the hills away.
For he who'd seek
A velvet cheek,
He rides not with me to-day."

When Mary came down the next morning, she was still in a fine little glow of indignation, she did not know exactly at what. Mrs. Treherne greeted her with a corresponding glow of delight.

"Well now, Miss Weymouth," she said, "it is a thousand pities you didn't hear my concert last night."

"Your concert?" repeated Mary.

"Yes, all my own!" said the good landlady, beaming. "'Twas while you were down to Cap'n Avery's, I expect. The other boarder, he sat out on the porch and sung to me, as much as an hour. Oh, there! he does sing beautiful! You might go to a dozen concerts, and not hear anything as much to my mind. I sat inside the door, — I don't dare to sit right out in the air, for fear of rheumatism, — and he stood there by the rail, and — well, it was like a bird and an organ, both together. There! I did wish you were where you could have opportunity to hear too! How quiet you came in! I never heard a sound. But you're always quiet."

"Thank you!" said Mary. "Apparently you would like me better if I were noisy, Mrs. Treherne."

"Now, how quick you are!" said Mrs. Treherne.

But except for this little flutter, Mary was now very happy. The people of the village, finding that she was one of themselves, by descent at least, took her into their hearts and homes. Many a happy hour she spent sitting on an upturned boat with Captain Simon or Captain Price, listening to wild tales of storm and shipwreck, or to quieter stories of life on the island. The fishermen's wives, too, made her kindly welcome to their firesides. There was always a baby she could hold, or a skein of yarn to wind, or quilt pieces to sort; and sitting thus, she learned the story of many a brave, faithful life. She made the acquaintance of the Oldest Inhabitant, a sweet and gracious woman, crowned with all the beauty of age; and from her and Mrs. Treherne, always her good friend, she learned to know her own forebears as she could not have known them elsewhere than in this home where they had toiled, and struggled, and died.

But still, best of all, she loved to wander alone over the windy hills, and climb among the fantastic rocks, and sit beside the clamorous sea. And she was at home everywhere, and everywhere happy.

One morning, quite early, she was sitting beside Captain Price, watching the mending of his boat, and knitting a sock for Mrs. Price's new baby. They talked of the island, as usual; there was no other subject for Mary in these days.

"'There's good folks on the island!" Captain Price said, as he whittled pegs. "Take 'em by and large, they are good folks. Different, of course, different, — no two alike in the Lord's fish-nets, — but take what I see over on the main, — I've been about consid'able, — and what I see here, and give me the island every time. None of your pork and sunset fellows here."

"Captain Price, what *do* you mean?" asked Mary. "Pork and sunset?"

"Well, it's an expression, Miss Weymouth," responded the Captain, slowly. "It's not an elegant expression; maybe I shouldn't have used it, speaking to a lady, but it means something like this: Over on the main, you go into a factory, say; and you see a lot of fellows working away, and most of 'em's working good, and laying down and doing their durn — doing the best they know how. That's so, ain't it, here in New England?"

"Yes, indeed!" said Mary, heartily. "I am sure it is, Captain Price."

"Well, I observed so!" returned the Captain. "That's where my observations brought me to, in general. But here and there, in that same lot, you'll see one fellow, — pity if there should be two in one gang, — you'll see one who keeps settin' back from his work, and all the time reason good to give for it. He has to get a drink — you'd think they was fish, sometimes, — though any one on this island would heave 'em back into the water, — the way they drink. Or he wants to know what o'clock it is, or he's got a stitch in his back, or something or other. Whatever excuse he can get up, that man is always settin' back, and waitin' for the whistle to blow noon, and then for it to blow night. All he wants is to stop off work; and that man is spotted by the other men, and they call him a pork and sunset man. That means he ain't no good. Well, what I say is, we have none of that sort on this island, Miss Weymouth, and we don't want any."

"I should think not!" said Mary, smiling.

"Then, —" the Captain went on, sighting carefully along his peg,—"then there's the summer folks." He paused with a side glance at the young girl.

"Oh, you need not mind, Captain Price!" cried Mary, eagerly. "I am not a summer person, you know; nothing of the sort! I belong to the island, just as much as if I had been born here."

"That so?" said the Captain, with a slow, gratified smile. "Well, I'm pleased to hear ye say so. It's an honour to the island; or so I consider it. But these summer folks, now,"— he waved his hand towards a shadowy host, — Mary could almost see them trooping up from the schooner, with groans over their "bad chance" coming over,— "I don't hardly see what some of 'em come here for. Of course, there's those that every one on the island is glad to see, and sorry to see go, and hoping they'll come again. But the other kind,— who come to see some kind of show, it appears as if,— I have no desire for their acquaintance, Miss Weymouth, and I should be free to tell them so, if manners allowed. It's not agreeable for folks that have lived here all their days, and done as best was give them to know how,— it's not agreeable to be looked at as if they was some kind of Injun, or fust cousin to a moose. Now is it?"

Mary shook her head vehemently, and would have spoken, but the Captain went on with another wave of his hand.

"Go over to the main there, and nobody takes notice of ye, more'n of another person. No horns, or tails, as I know of, to an island man; pass in the crowd for a real person, every time. But come over here, and they stare at ye as if they expected ye to be blue. Perhaps 'tis because they are green!" he added, with a chuckle. "Now, they was a young man come here last summer. Green? why, grass was yeller beside him. He come here, and he was sea-sick, and home-sick, and love-sick, all three together."

"Poor thing!" cried Mary. "How pitiful!"

"Well, that is the word, Miss Weymouth!" said the Captain. "Pitiful he was; and took a lot of photographs, and tried to make up to Susetta Harlan. Wrote poetry, I'm told, about an island maiden. Why, he didn't know one end of a fish from the other, Susetta said; and asked her if a cod's sounds were melodious! Well, there's all kinds!" He meditated for a moment, then, brightening up, added:

"That's a very different sort of young man you've got down to Mis' Treherne's, now. There's what I call a gentleman, if

I see him carrying a hod on a ladder. Chock full of sense, with an eye in his head; and so pleasant, you feel like 'hurrah boys!' every time you hear him speak. And understands a boat."

On this final word he paused. "There was na moore to say!"

Mary saw that a reply was expected from her.

"Oh — yes!" she said, hastily. "That is, I hardly know — but, Captain Price, I should think you would be jealous of every one who comes here. Why, I hate them, myself, and I have only been here a few weeks; but it seems half a lifetime, and I cannot bear the thought of going away. How can *you* ever bear to go to the main, — to go inland, and lose sight of the sea? I should think you would stifle for want of your own air."

The Captain gave a short laugh.

"Maybe you are right, Miss Weymouth," he said, slowly, "but we don't always feel that way ourselves. It's different, you see, coming for a spell, from what it is to summer and winter right along. Why, I remember a time — good many years ago 'tis now — when I got downright sick of the island, and the sea, and the whole thing of it. I suppose likely I wasn't over and above well; anyhow, it come over me strong that I'd had enough sea for one spell. Seemed to me that if I could only get away off up country somewheres, out of sight and sound of it, and lay under an apple-tree and eat apples, — all the apples I wanted, — it seemed to me that would be about as near heaven as I could imagine this side of Jordan."

"Oh!" cried Mary. "Oh, how strange! And did you go, Captain Price?"

"I went," said the Captain, nodding with deliberate emphasis. "I went over to the main, and I went up country quite a ways, and hired out to a farmer. Well! 'twas a place shut in like a box, with mountings all round it; over Camden

ON THE BEACH. 47

way, but inland, you see. The man was as close as a hungry lobster. We lived on salt fish that wouldn't be given to no island pig that was desired to fatten. I never see a pound of fresh fish while I was there. Rank fish, and pork — and no sunset," he added, with a twinkle, "because of it's being shut off by the mountings. It was a terrible place."

"And the apples!" cried Mary. "Did you have the apples, all you wanted?"

The Captain laughed again, his short, dry laugh.

"The apples were green when I went there," he said; "and green apples never suited my internal legislature. Soon as I saw one that looked friendly, I ate it; and he saw me, and threatened to put me in jail if he caught me with another."

"Oh! oh! the miserable wretch! And then, Captain?"

"I went away next day," said the Captain. "I went and bought a peck of apples of the man on the next farm, and came and sat down on the old man's fence and ate 'em, and threw the cores into his dooryard. He was proper mad, but he didn't dare to say anything, for he knew I was mad too, fighting mad. Then I came back to the island. I'd had enough of the main for one while."

They were silent for a moment, each enjoying the story in his own way. Then the old man said:

"And you do feel to regard the island as your belonging to it? Now that is a pleasant thing, surely! That gives pleasure — to the mind. And you've been about, pretty much nigh all over it, have ye? Have you been in the Black Woods, I wonder?"

No, Mary had not heard of the Black Woods. Where were they, that she might find them at once, this morning, this moment?

Captain Price laid his pipe beside his jack-knife, pulled out a bit of string, and made an elaborate chart of the island.

"'Tis quite a piece on from here!" he said. "You have to go round the big bog, remember; you couldn't get through it, no way in the world."

"I see! I understand!" cried Mary, her eyes shining with the joy of the explorer. "Here I strike off to the northeast; yes, I am sure I can find the way."

"I don't hardly know!" said the Captain. "I don't hardly know as you'd better try it alone, young lady. The woods are thick, mighty thick. We can't have you getting lost, you know. That would never do! Suppose you wait and let me go with you, when this rheumatism lets up a little in my joints!"

Mary thanked him, and said that would be delightful. Then suddenly recollecting some important business that must take her directly back to the Influence, she bade the Captain good-by, and thanked him so prettily for all the pleasant things he had told her, that she left the good man in a little glow of pleasure. He watched her as she took her way up the beach, noting her light step and the pretty way she carried her head. "That's what I call a lady!" said the Captain to his pipe.

In less than an hour Mary was on her way to the Black Woods.

CHAPTER IV.

THE BLACK WOODS.

MARY went by dale and down, her heart full of joy. She was to find a new place, one whose existence she had not suspected. She had gone around the island on the rocks, and across it over the hills, but this place, as the Captain described it, lay hidden behind a high shoulder that she had not yet climbed. She had always been stopped by the great moss, the quaking bog that spread its broad, treacherous surface of tufted green well-nigh across the middle of the island. She had not known of this way round; now she was sure of her path, and she trod on air. But when she came near, and left the green, smiling meadow, and saw the woods rising before her black and grim, her face grew grave, and the little song died on her lips. This was no place to laugh about!

Spruce and fir, fir and spruce, knotted and tangled and twisted together in dense masses. The trees never of great height, but often of enormous girth, stunted giants, reaching out massive, distorted limbs to lock with their neighbours'. Every tree was bearded with moss, and crusted thick with black and gray lichens. Here and there was a dead one, bleached and naked, unable to fall, the stark form held upright by the close ranks of the living.

An awful place, Mary thought; but how beautiful! how unearthly lovely! The rocks thrust themselves up through the thin soil in fantastic shapes, the gnomes that watched the hidden treasures of this fairy forest; and they were clad in the fairies' fatal green, moss so rich and so delicate that Mary could not find words for it, could only stroke and pat it with murmurs of delight.

"*Perhaps* this is the most beautiful of all!" she said. "I don't say positively, but I must think about it. Oh! and *will* you look?" she broke off short, for on the rock at her foot the bright moss was all embroidered with rose-colour, fine, quaint patterns, traced in tiny buttons of pale pink coral. Fungi, were they? what a stupid language English was, to have no lovely word for so lovely a thing!

Progress was necessarily slow through the Black Woods. Mary's eyes were in constant peril from the interlacing twigs. She had often to force her way along, taking her whole strength to it, bending back the stubborn branches, like twisted rods of iron, that barred her way at every step. Once she came very near her end. So absorbed was she in fighting her way through these ranks of silent, bearded sentinels, that she did not hear the sound that was growing nearer and louder at every step, till suddenly light shone in upon her; the woods broke off short, and the rocks fell away from her feet, and there was the sea leaping and shouting a hundred feet below.

It may be that this rather shook our Mary's nerve; or it may be, on the other hand, that she grew careless, and overconfident. However it was, she had not gone very far back from the break in the woods when suddenly her foot caught in a wandering loop of fir-root. She stumbled, tried to save herself, and finally came heavily to the ground.

She was stunned for a moment; then, her eyes clearing, she tried to rise hastily, but sank back with a cry of pain.

She had sprained her ankle.

"What shall I do now?" said Mary Weymouth.

She was a resolute girl, and at first she was contented with feeling positively sure that she would get home somehow. She *must!*

She tried to stand, but found it impossible. She tried to hop on the other foot, but this made the pain so distracting that she cried out again, and sat for some time rocking backward and forward, like a hurt child.

"Well, then, I must creep; that's all!" she said; and she started on her hands and knees, being nearly three miles from home, in the middle of a tangled wilderness.

Any one who has tried to drag a sprained ankle through a rough forest will have some idea of what she was attempting; any one who has not, is not recommended to try it.

After ten minutes of agony, Mary had made a progress of three rods. She became aware that if she persisted she should soon faint, and there would be an end of it; so she gave up the battle, and set her back against a tree, and waited.

At first she could not think. All the world was throbbing with anguish, and all that anguish centred in her ankle, which was punishing her cruelly for the treatment it had received. But when the pain quieted a little, she considered her position. She was nearly three miles from home, as has been said. It had taken all her strength to make her way through this stubborn wood, when her strength was rejoicing through every limb of her; now she was disabled. No one was likely to come this way; it was out of the track of the island people, a place given up to savagery, which busy men were glad to let alone. What would become of her?

"I certainly don't want to die here!" said Mary. She laughed as she spoke, but it was rather a dreary little laugh, and the trees did not take it up. She wondered what time it was; she had forgotten her watch. Near dinner-time, surely, for she was hungry. Well, Mrs. Treherne would wonder why she did not come to dinner, but she would not take the alarm till near nightfall, being used to her going off on long excursions. When it came towards supper-time, the good landlady would be frightened indeed, and no doubt there would be a search-party organised, and in due course of time they would find her. After all, the island was not so very large; yet it might very well be that this would be the last place they would think of searching. Captain Price was going off fishing at noon,— he had told her so; and no one else would know of the talk they had had, and how he had told her about these horrible woods.

Well, and if she had to spend the night here; what of it? She would be very hungry, of course. Dear me! she was very hungry now! but people could not starve in one night. And she would not freeze, — though the nights were pretty cool for sleeping out. And — there was nothing to hurt her.

This last assurance came more slowly than the others. Mary looked around, in a mute appeal to the trees. She had always thought, with her favourite Stevenson, that trees were among the most friendly people in the world; but these trees were not friendly. They seemed to press round her, grim and unhelpful; there was no tremor of sympathy in any smallest twig; no sigh of compassion moved their bushy tops; all was stark and silent.

"Miserable comforters are ye all!" said poor Mary.

If there were even a squirrel, it would be something! but there was no squirrel.

In spite of her determination to be steadfast and cheerful, Mary found herself already fancying how it would be when night fell, in this grim desolation: the black trees blotted out by the deeper blackness; hunger, cold, fear!

Fear! she had hardly thought the word, when it seemed to possess the air, — the whole place. Weak as she was with pain and weariness, fear seized her, and common sense shrank away appalled.

Who knew what creatures there might be lurking in this savage place? Might not this be the last resort of those beasts that civilisation had driven from the mainland? Bears, — panthers, perhaps! and what was that Indian Devil, about which she had once read a terrible story? Would not any such beast, lingering unguessed in these deathly solitudes, smell her out at whatever distance, and come creeping — creeping —

Ah! heaven! what was that?

The silence had been absolute, dead, noted only by her own heart-beats. But now, far off, the branches crackled, the dry leaves rustled. Something was moving through the wood! Something alive was coming nearer — nearer!

Mary's heart stopped; then sprang up wildly and beat to suffocation. She forgot the pain for an instant, and tried once more to rise to her feet; but the ankle turned under her, and she fell again. Now, in mortal terror, her hands clasped, her breath coming and going in short, quick pants, the girl waited — for what?

Nearer, the crackling, the rustling and rending! This was no harmless little wild-wood creature that was making its way through the dense forest; this was powerful strength that was tearing the stubborn branches apart. How should she bear it? What prayer could give her strength?

Hark! oh, mercy! hark! What was that?

For over the crashing of branches, clear, and high, and sweet, rose now another sound; and hearing it, Mary Weymouth put her face down in her hands, and wept, and laughed, and wept again, that it was shame to hear her.

"Toreador, prends garde!"

"Help!" she cried; and she started at her own voice, which sounded like a stranger's. "John Harvard, help!"

There was a brief exclamation of surprise; then more crackling and rending; and in a few minutes a very surprised young man stood looking down upon a much confused young woman.

"Miss Smith," said John Harvard. "I beg your pardon! Did you call me?"

"My name is not Smith!" said Mary, faintly.

"Of course it isn't!" cried the young man, flushing a very honest red. "Awfully stupid of me! I — I saw Smith College on the trunk, don't you know?"

He paused a moment, giving her an opening to mention her real name; but she said nothing, and he went on more stiffly, "Is there anything I can do for you?"

"I have sprained my ankle!" said Mary. "I cannot — walk —"

"Great Scott!" said John Harvard. "Oh, I say, I'm awfully sorry! Let me look at it! I am a surgeon," he added, as Mary looked up in feeble, but manifest indignation.

"I — don't believe it!" she said. "You are an undergraduate!"

The young man gave a short laugh. "I was once!" he said. "I graduated at the medical school a year ago, and have been in the hospital ever since. Come!" He was kneeling beside her now, and spoke authoritatively. "Let me see — I should think so! Did it not occur to you to take off your boot at once? Now I shall have to cut it. What a shame to spoil a good boot like this!"

He spoke in an injured tone. Out came his knife, and in a few minutes the mangled boot lay on the ground.

"Now take off the stocking," he commanded, "while I go for some water. It will be easier for you getting home if it is well bandaged."

Mary wanted to say, "I wish I had not called you!" but it was becoming difficult to talk; and the stocking was off when the young surgeon returned, with a folding cup full of water. Her handkerchief was next demanded, torn in strips together with his own; and then came a moment of exquisite relief, as the cool, wet bandage was wound round and round, quickly, delicately, strongly.

"Safety-pin!" said John Harvard, as if they grew on every tree in the woods. "Hold on — I have one!" and so he had, under the lapel of his coat. Mary wondered what kind of girl had pinned the flower there.

"Now!" he said. "Let us see if we can stand. Lean all your weight on me — so! Ah! just as I feared!"

Mary rose to her feet, obedient to the strong hand that raised her; stood for a moment wavering, clinging to the young man's arm, — then the world turned black, revolved once, and vanished.

"Great Scott!" said John Harvard, as he caught her.

Mary was rocking in a cradle, on an uneven floor. No! she was in a boat, and the sea was choppy. No! she was riding on a camel. The motion was pleasanter than she had supposed it; but how did camels come to be used in the woods —

Here she came to herself with a violent start, and became aware of a gray shoulder directly above her, and still above, a brown head bobbing serenely in time to the slow, regular strides of its owner.

"Oh! Oh, Mr. Harvard!" cried Mary, now fully awake. "How can you? oh, put me down, please!"

"*Mr. Harvard* is good," said the young man, "and well deserved; but as to putting you down, just wait a minute, till we get out of this boggy place."

"You shouldn't!" Mary protested, feebly.

"Did you want to stay there?" was the reply.

Mary murmured something about a wheelbarrow (there is no horse on the island), and was briefly bidden to look about her.

"As soon as we get clear of the trees,"

said John Harvard, " I will put you down, and go and get Captain Avery and a chair, or a hammock, or something; then we can get you home comfortably. Nothing could have been got into that place where I found you. Am I holding you pretty well? Are you dreadfully uncomfortable?"

Mary was not, and said so, trying to feel as grateful as she ought.

" Used to carrying lame sister!" was the brief explanation. And then nothing more was said till he set her gently down in a little open space, on a tuft of moss under a spreading tree.

" You must be quite exhausted!" said Mary, remorsefully, looking up as the young man stretched his cramped arms and shook himself.

" Not a bit!" was the cheery answer. " Been training all the spring with a crew. Ha! Now — you are all right here for half an hour — Miss Smith?"

" All right, Mr. Harvard — thank you!"

Then their eyes met, and Mary found herself laughing helplessly, whether she would or no.

"It *is* funny!" she said, ruefully.

"Isn't it!" said John Harvard. "Awfully funny!" and off he went across the hill.

CHAPTER V.

SOUVENT FEMME VARIE.

"AND I must say, Mary Weymouth, I think you are a very ungrateful girl!"

It was Mrs. Treherne who spoke. She had dropped the "Miss" some time before, in speaking to Mary; had they not discovered that the young girl was niece to her third cousin, once removed?

The two women were sitting in the pleasant parlour, Mary on the sofa, Mrs. Treherne in the rocking-chair.

"Ungrateful!" repeated Mrs. Treherne. "Here has Mr.—"

"I tell you I don't *want* to know his name!" broke in Mary, petulantly.

"Well, if you are not contrary!" sighed

the good landlady. "Here has he been as kind as kind, and tended your foot, and kept you from having a serious lameness, like as not, to say nothing of his bringing you out of those awful woods, where you might have been to this day, if it hadn't been for him, — and now you won't ask him to come into the sitting-room."

"Oh! how you do *tease* me, Mrs. Treherne!" cried Mary, turning fretfully on her sofa.

"It's not my sitting-room, as I have told you twenty times. He is as free to come here as I am. Why doesn't he come, then, if he wants to?"

"That's foolish talk!" said Mrs. Treherne. "You know as well as I do that he won't come unless you ask him. I never saw folks behave so foolish in my life. There!"

"Then he can stay out!" said Mary.

She was silent, listening to the sound of regular footsteps outside, pacing up and down the verandah. The steps were accompanied by a cheerful whistle, but the rain was pattering on the windows, and the wind whistled drearily through the cracks. A northeaster was setting in, and it was not probably pleasant out there. Mary threw an angry glance at the landlady. Why could not one be let alone for a little while? Her mind went back over the scenes of the past week. She hurried over the adventure in the wood; she did not care to dwell upon it; besides, there was no danger of her forgetting it. But she thought of the succeeding days, when she had been so feverish and wretched, and the young surgeon had never failed to come twice a day to look at her bandages, and to sit beside her for a few minutes, full of cheery talk and pleasant stories. He never alluded to the past, nor to the future. One would think he had never seen her before; that she was simply a new patient, and — to judge from his manner — rather an interesting one. He called her Miss Smith, and she called him Mr. Harvard, with perfect composure, as if neither had known any other name. It certainly was foolish, but —

Well, and then what had happened? Mary hardly knew. Had she fancied one day that the look in his eyes was too kind, the pressure of his hand too cordial, as he greeted her? and had she drawn back in consequence, veiled her own eyes with coldness, answered indifferently the friendly greeting? Possibly! one could not always keep exactly the right shade of tone in one's voice; but surely that was not sufficient reason for his withdrawing absolutely into his shell, and never coming near her since she began to come down-stairs. She didn't believe she had been so disagreeable as all that; and even if she had —

The girl shut her eyes; and when she did so, she saw a brown head bobbing above hers, and heard a voice ask. "Do

I hold you pretty well? Are you dreadfully uncomfortable?"

She opened her eyes promptly; she must be still weak, or this ridiculous thing would not go on,— and she heard the strong, steady tread outside, and the cheerful whistle, and the rain pattering down. It was actually pouring now. Oh, if one had to be one's own scapegoat!

She threw another black look at the landlady; then leaned forward, and, as the steps drew near, knocked on the window by the head of her sofa.

The steps stopped. Mary knocked again. "Won't you come in?" she said.

"All right!" was the answer; and the next minute the young man entered, six foot of sunburnt health and cheeriness. Mary had a moment of exasperation. Why should he be striding about, and looking like that, when she was on this tiresome sofa?

"Oh!" she said, rather unamiably.

"Mrs. Treherne wanted you to come in; she was afraid you would get wet."

Then, seeing the swift change in his face, and flushing scarlet at her own rudeness, she cried out: "No! that isn't it at all! We are tired to death of each other; we want to be amused. Won't you sit down — please — and amuse us?"

People said that Mary Weymouth had the most winning smile in the world, when she chose to make use of it; certainly, John Harvard did not even try to resist it. He sat down by the fire, and looked at the young girl with friendly eyes. "How is the ankle to-day?" he said.

"That doesn't amuse me!" said Mary. "The ankle is very much better, — thanks! That ointment is really wonderful. Did you get it from a witch?"

He nodded. "She lives over by Green Point. Her name is Hazel, and she has tufts of yellow hair growing on her arms;

also, she has an extraordinary bark. Does this amuse you?"

"Pretty well!" said Mary, laughing. "But I would rather hear a story. Have you a story of your own, or are you a needy knife-grinder?"

"You describe me accurately," said the young man, gravely. And he added, with an odd little inflection in his voice, "My story is just beginning."

"I don't understand a word you two are saying," said Mrs. Treherne.

"Oh! but it is you who have the stories, Mrs. Treherne," said Mary, turning with animation to her hostess. "Tell us a story; please do! Tell us about this house. Didn't you say it was the oldest house on the island? There must be stories about it."

"Well, I don't know," said Mrs. Treherne; and she pondered a moment.

"I've told you about the naming of it, and all that." Assured that she had not, the good lady counted her stitches and settled herself comfortably in her chair.

"Yes," she said, "this is the oldest house on the island, surely. It is called the Influence. They used to name the houses in those days, same as they did ships and folks; and there was a great to-do over the raising of this one. My great-grandfather, Polwarth, built it, and his daughter christened it, and made the posy."

"Oh, how delightful!" cried Mary. "Tell us all about the christening."

"I wasn't there," said Mrs. Treherne, with a twinkle. "But they do say it was a great occasion. Peggy Polwarth was the handsomest girl anywhere in these parts, island or main, and folks came from far and near to 'tend the christening. There *was* a story of a boat coming over from Matinicus with three young men aboard, and all of them in love with Peggy, and they quarrelling about which should have her, and upsetting the boat, and all three drowned; but I never believed that myself. Anyhow, Peggy came down to the raising, in a white gown and flowers in her hair; and she ran up the ladder like a squirrel, and stood on the ridge-pole, and walked the len'th of it with her two arms stretched out, — so't folks was scared to death she'd fall and break her neck. She was a terrible lively girl. But she didn't fall; and she broke the bottle, and she said like this:

> "'This is a fine frame,
>   Raised in a pleasant spot.
> May God bless the owner,
>   And all he has got!
> It shall be called "The Influence,"
>   And the "Landlady's Delight;"
> It was raised on Thursday,
>   A little before night.'"

"Oh, what a delightful thing!" sighed Mary. "To have it really true, and to be actually living in the house! And *has* it been your delight, Mrs. Treherne?"

"Humph!" said Mrs. Treherne. "That depends upon the kind of guests I have. It takes all kinds to make folks."

"And how about the 'Influence'?" asked John Harvard. "That seems to me very interesting. What do you suppose was in the young girl's mind? And it would be curious if one could trace any influence — any similarity in the lives of the people who lived in this house."

Mrs. Treherne glanced at him under her eyebrows.

"Folks used to call it 'Courtship Castle,' one while," she said, quietly. "There's been more marriages from this house than from any three on the island."

"Oh!" said John Harvard, thoughtfully.

At this moment a bell tinkled in the distance. The young man looked up and sighed.

"There is my supper-bell!" he said. "Dear me! This fire is altogether too pleasant to leave, — to say nothing of the company."

Mrs. Treherne reflected a moment, knitting rapidly. "I've been meaning to say to you and Miss — "

"Smith!" said Mary, quickly.

"Well, I declare!" said Mrs. Treherne. "I've been meaning to tell you both, — my girl thinks she can't get so many meals, right along, so. She isn't over strong, and I can't have her fall sick, with the summer just beginning. Suppose you both take your tea with me tonight! 'Twould be an accommodation, I assure you; and I get real lonesome sometimes, sitting there all alone."

"Why, of course, Mrs. Treherne!" cried Mary. "How thoughtless, how inconsiderate we have been!"

"Awfully stupid!" murmured John Harvard.

"Thank you!" said Mary, demurely.

"Oh, I say!" cried John Harvard. "You know what I meant! And — and

I think Mrs. Treherne is right. It's awfully poky eating alone, don't you think? Do let us have supper all together!"

"And it is my supper, too!" said Mrs. Treherne, smiling. "Your bell rang half an hour ago, sir, and you never heard it."

"You don't say so!" said the young man. "The world is so full of a number of things—"

"Oh, you love Stevenson?" cried Mary, her eyes shining.

"Well, I hope so!" said the young man. Hereupon ensued a sudden eager babble of both voices, which was unintelligible to Mrs. Treherne, waiting with Mary's crutches in her hand. She heard "Kidnapped," "The Master—"

"Oh, but the 'Ebb-tide'!"

"You know 'Underwoods'?"

"By heart! From cover to cover!"

"I, too! Oh! 'Our Lady of the Snows'—"

"But the Fables,— nothing like them!—"

"Your supper will be as cold as a stone!" said the landlady, plaintively. "And it is a good supper, if I do say it."

"I am fed on proper meat!" cried John Harvard, gaily. His eyes danced, and the girl's shone in glad response. It seemed as if some chord had been touched, some common bond discovered, which destroyed with a touch the barrier between them.

"What are these for?" said John Harvard, pointing to the crutches. "You don't need those things any more, surely. Take my arm! I am quite sure it will be all you need."

Mrs. Treherne laid down the crutches, and followed quietly; they seemed to have forgotten her. And they all had a feast of joy, — and lobsters, — and there were no more solitary meals at the Influence.

CHAPTER VI.

THE ROCK HOUSE.

AGAIN it was closing in for a rainy evening; but Mary did not mind the rain this time. She had had a delightful day, and a delightful evening was before her. The ankle was well, and she and her former enemy had been off on an exploring tour together. Great as was the joy of rambling alone among the mighty hills and the wild rocks, Mary found it to be surpassed by the pleasure of doing the same thing in agreeable company. A strong hand always ready to help her over the dikes and chasms, a quick eye that took in every anemone in the rock-pools, every flower on the uplands; a hearty, ready will to see everything, do everything, enjoy everything, — and withal a manifest pleasure in her society, — what maiden would not prefer this to solitude, if she were in any degree right-minded? Mary had been wrong-minded; she acknowledged that; and now it was really much more sensible to be friendly and — and nice to this young man. They might never meet again after this summer; their paths would lie far apart; she would try to leave a pleasant impression on his mind.

So they had had a joyful morning about Gull Rock, and now she was looking forward to a cheerful evening by the fireside, with Mrs. Treherne knitting and rocking, and John Harvard reading "Pride and Prejudice" aloud. Dear Elizabeth! dear Darcy! she had been so clever to bring them with her!

Singing a gay little song, she ran down-stairs when the tea-bell rang. Mrs. Treherne was sitting alone at the table, looking rather grave.

"Where is Mr. Harvard?" asked Mary.

"Dear me!" said Mrs. Treherne. "I do wish he'd come back! I feel real worried about him; there!"

"Why! what — where is he?" cried Mary, looking anxious in her turn.

"Word came about an hour ago, while you were resting, that a child was sick up to the Rock House, as they call it. It's a little old house, about a mile up from the street. The man who lives there is a newcomer, a Norwegian. He hasn't been there more'n a few months, and his wife is sick, and has this babe, about six months old. Don't you remember my telling you, Mary?"

"Oh! yes, yes!" cried Mary, remorsefully. "And I was only thinking of myself and my ankle, and forgot all about it. Well, and what else?"

"Why, the man is cantankerous!" said Mrs. Treherne. "One woman and another has tried to help them, but he drinks,

I guess, and there can't no one stand his temper. I guess his wife has a hard time of it, poor soul. To-day she sent word that the baby was sick, and wouldn't I come? but I couldn't, for I promised to sit up to-night with Mis' Mays. She's failing fast, and her folks are worn out watching. I never did see so much sickness on the island as there is now. It seems as if every family had their hands full; and no doctor, and — well, Mr. Harvard said right off, he'd go, though he had a cold, and 'tis a dismal place up there. So off he went, and that's the last I've heard. I hated to have him go every way. We do aim to care for our folks well, here on the island; but these people seem to be by themselves, some way of it. The man's off fishing, and I don't know whether the woman is able to do for herself and the child, let alone Mr. Harvard, — it does seem foolish to call him out of his name, good as he is, but you will have your way! And not a bite of anything to eat since noon, and may be there half the night! There! I am discouraged!"

Mary had listened in silence, sipping her tea and eating her bread and butter. Now she said, quietly:

"I will go up there, Mrs. Treherne. If you will get me a basket, I will take up Mr. Harvard's supper, and stay and help a little. Oh, you needn't look surprised!" she added. "I know a good deal about sickness, and I am used to babies, and I know the way to the house. So make up a good little basket, there's a dear, and I will be off as soon as I have finished my griddle-cakes. I suppose you couldn't send him any of those? They do look so good!"

She spoke cheerfully, but with decision; and Mrs. Treherne, after remonstrating properly against her going out on such a night, was glad to yield. A basket was packed with tea and sugar, a bottle of milk, bread and butter, and good Mrs.

Treherne slipped in a pot of raspberry jam, with apologies.

" 'Twill make it heavy, I know," she said, "but he does set by it, and I don't know as it weighs so *very* much."

"I think I can stagger under it!" said Mary, laughing. She had taken off her pretty house dress, and put on the familiar short blue skirt and jacket. Over her shoulders she threw a short rough cape with a hood, fixed her Tam-o'-Shanter firmly on her head, and felt ready for anything.

"Won't you take an umbrella?" said Mrs. Treherne. "Child, you'll be wet through before you get there."

"Not I!" said Mary. "My skirt and cloak are waterproof; so is Tammy; basket and lantern are all I can manage. Good-bye! and don't worry, if I should not get back till morning."

She laughed at Mrs. Treherne's exclamation of horror, and stepped bravely out into the lashing rain. The lantern swung to her rapid steps, throwing its gleams to right and left, and lighting up the rocks, gay with orange lichens, that bordered the steep, crooked village street. Not a soul was out this wild night. A body was, however, for half-way down the street a great head flashed out of the darkness before her, and she almost ran into David, the village bull. David spent his peaceful days wandering up and down the village, and was now probably going somewhere to bed. Mary recoiled with a little shriek, and ran swiftly past the huge creature. She did not like bulls. David was generally amiable, but the day before he had taken more notice of her red scarf than was pleasant. Yes, and John Harvard had taken him by his horns, and turned him round, and then with a friendly kick sent him lumbering off towards the post-office.

How it did rain! Up the hill now, by the schoolhouse; then to the left, through Captain Janeway's yard; opening and shutting all the queer little gates, jumping from one level to another, crossing the tiny stream, which raged furiously in its bed, like an angry baby. The smell of the fish — for she knew exactly where Captain Janeway dried his fish — guided her to the last gate of all, and once past this, she was out on the north down, with the sea bellowing below, and the wind and rain swooping and shrieking at her above.

It was a wild night! Had she known how wild —

Yes! She would have come just the same. Was she not descended from island people? This was her home, the home of her heart.

Here she stepped on a sheep, huddled asleep under a point of rock, and came near falling headlong over the cliff. The sheep rose and fled, remonstrating. "Well, I like that," said Mary, "when you came near killing me!"

On she went, the storm buffeting and tearing at her, the surf thundering beneath her feet. She began to realise what she had undertaken. A moment's faintness seized her, at the thought of that white, boiling waste below, which she could not see. If she had fallen — she faltered. Had she overrated her strength? would she be able to reach the house?

Then there came to her mind a word of the Poet-Master whom she loved, — "The bright face of danger — "

She shook her head resolutely, and pressed bravely on; and almost the next moment, rounding a point of rock, she saw a light not far off, and knew it was the goal she sought. A few minutes more of battling against a wall that was alive, and that bit and scratched and screamed at her, — and breathless and dripping, Mary stood at the door of the Rock House.

The young man whom we have known as John Harvard had been having a very uncomfortable two hours. He had started at once on hearing of the sick baby; with a little sigh, to be sure, and a glance at the pleasure he was leaving behind, yet with a steady, cheerful gaze, bent on the duty before him. He was rather a good fellow, this John Harvard. Reaching the house, he found the woman — a Norwegian, who spoke little English — suffering from a sharp attack of pleurisy. He took the crying child from her arms, and sent her promptly to bed. Then, when he had mixed and administered the proper remedies, he considered what to do next. The baby was wailing, the woman moaning, the fire gone out.

"When in doubt, fill the kettle!" said John Harvard, remembering his mother's admonitions. He laid the baby in the cradle. It screamed lustily, but he hardened his heart, and filled the kettle and built up a roaring fire. Then he took the baby again, and observed it carefully. The poor little creature was behaving very like the Duchess's baby in "Alice," doubling itself up and straightening itself out again, screaming violently all the time. When he laid it on his shoulder and walked up and down the room with it, the screams quieted a little. He felt the little hands and head; no fever! The baby face was scarlet with crying, but the limbs were plump and firm, and the lungs were certainly in superb condition. Poor little thing! It was sobbing quietly now, and John Harvard was aware of a queer sensation about his heart, as he felt the velvet cheek against his own. Poor little beggar! it was a shame to have to be a baby, and to have pains too!

Then, somehow, he found himself thinking of that other head that had rested on his shoulder, not so many days ago. It had been heavier than the baby's, but not at all too heavy. And how pale and lovely she looked, with the long lashes on her cheek!

And the way the colour came flooding

back when she opened her eyes! Ah! — well, — one didn't have such luck twice!

What was the matter with this baby, anyhow? Nothing very serious, or it could not look like this. Now that it was quiet, he would lay it in the cradle, and see how the mother was getting on. But the moment he put the child down, it screamed and shrieked so violently, that the poor woman woke from the doze into which she had fallen, and moaned in concert.

"Wife dying up-stairs, mad dog down!" quoted John Harvard. "Are we to keep this up all night?"

He took the baby up again, and resumed his march. Up and down, up and down! Perhaps he could get it to sleep! What did one sing to a baby? "Toreador" would only send it broad awake.

He began to croon softly a little old French song.

> "Quand j'ai vu Madeline
> Pour la première fois,
> Elle gravait la colline,
> Je descendais du bois.
> En robe du Dimanche,
> En guimpe et jupe blanche,
> Elle allait sous les branches.
> Que les beaux jours sont courts!"

But it was the second verse that had been haunting him, ever since that day in the woods.

> "Pour aller au village,
> Le chemin fait un pli;
> Et la veille un orage
> D'eau l'avait tout rempli.
> Souriante et legère,
> Je l'enlevai de terre;
> Elle se laissa faire.
> Que les beaux jours sont courts!"

Circumstances different, result the same!

> "'Je l'enlevai de terre;
> Elle se laissa faire'—

because she couldn't help herself, poor dar — oh, come, this will never do!

Baby, what are you about? Almost asleep? That's good!

"'Que les beaux jours sont courts!'"

"By Jove, aren't they! And that brute of a Tom coming to pick me up next week. Well, I won't go, anyhow."

But then — Tom might come ashore — oh, bother Tom!

"Hush, baby! hush! — Better now, ma'am? That's right! As soon as I can put the baby down, I'll get you some milk, or gruel, or something. Hush — hush — baby — bye! Hush — hush — oh, Great Scott!"

For he had thought the baby sound asleep, and had laid it once more in the cradle; and here it was yelling like a little demon, and twisting itself into hard knots.

The young man caught up the child again, and struck out once more in a kind of despair. How long would this last? Till the child grew up? There was a man who carried a calf till it grew to be an ox —

But just at this moment, while the baby was screaming, the mother sighing, and John Harvard stalking with tragic brows, — Hamlet in the nursery, — the door opened.

As if blown in by the gale, came a light figure, dripping, breathless, with glowing cheeks and shining eyes. So lightly, quickly, the girl came, the young man thought her for an instant a part of his dream. " Souriante et legère ! "

But no ! She was real. She was setting down a basket, hanging up her wet cloak, warming her hands at the fire, and all the time smiling at him — oh, no one else in the world knew how to smile !

"Oh, I say !" cried John Harvard.

In two minutes the basket was unpacked. In five, the gruel was on the stove, a plate on the table, and Mary was holding out her arms for the baby.

"Oh, I say !" said John Harvard again. " You're awfully good ! I'm so glad you have come ! But how could you come in this storm? You ought not to have stirred out of doors. Are you sure he isn't too heavy for you? I can't make out what is the matter with the child!" he continued; and the relief in his tone, as he gave up his charge, was almost comic.

"You see,— of course I've had very little experience, and most of that surgical, — casual wards and all that,— and I cannot tell! He doesn't seem to be in pain, till I put him into the cradle, and then he screams like — like — oh, I am so glad you have come!"

He sat down with a deep sigh of content, and looked at Mary, and then at the raspberry jam. He was a healthy and vigorous youth, and it was an hour and more past supper-time.

Mary sat down by the fire, with the baby in her arms; she cooed and murmured to it, and the baby looked up at her, with its pretty eyes all red and swollen with crying.

"My lamb!" said Mary. "My little poor, sweet lamb! What did hurt it, a kitty baby?"

She laid the child on its back; it screamed, and grew purple in the face. She turned it over on its face; the screams died away into moans, into faint sobs, then stopped altogether.

"There!" said John Harvard. "That's the way it has been acting ever since I came. Most extraordinary thing!"

"I should think so!" said Mary, quietly.

She patted the child; she felt it all over with swift, light fingers. "My lamb!" she said again. "It was a wicked, wicked shame, so it was!" and she drew out, and held up in the firelight — a pin!

"Right in his precious back!" she said. "The only wonder is that the child hasn't had a fit!"

"Great Scott!" said John Harvard.

When the two started on their homeward walk together, mother and child were both sleeping sweetly. The father had come home, sober and conciliatory. The rain and wind still continued, but it was a joyful pæan that they roared and shouted. A glorious night for a walk, both young people agreed. With Mary on his arm, John Harvard thought lightly of the prince of the powers of the air. Once, indeed, the desire to kiss her came upon him so strongly, that in repressing it he pressed her arm unconsciously.

"Oh!" cried Mary. "What is the matter? Is it the bull?"

"No, no! nothing!" said the young man, in confusion. "Nothing at all! I had — a pain ; that's all."

"A pain? Oh! Where?"

"Somewhere about the heart!" said John Harvard. "It's of no consequence; I often have them. That is, it's of a great deal of consequence, but no matter!"

"Oh!" said Mary. "I thought perhaps it was a pin!"

CHAPTER VII.

"QUE LES BEAUX JOURS SONT COURTS."

THE next morning was Sunday. The mail schooner had come in late the night before, and a little pile of letters lay by each plate on the breakfast-table. John Harvard opened his, and gloomed black as thunder. Mary opened hers, and sighed. Last, Mrs. Treherne, after pouring out the coffee, and presuming that the drop-cakes were not fit to eat, turned to her own budget, and, reading one, uttered an exclamation of surprise.

"I declare, I'm sorry!" she said. "'Tis time, to be sure, but I surely am sorry." Then, as the others looked up in wonder — "My first batch of boarders comes day after to-morrow!" she said.

"Well, that's some comfort!" said John Harvard. Mrs. Treherne looked at him open-eyed, and he added, quickly:

"I have just heard that they are coming for me to-morrow. An awful bore — but if a lot of people are coming —"

"I have my summons, too!" said Mary, looking up with heightened colour. "My father is coming to New York, and wants me to meet him there. I must go back by Tuesday's boat."

A blank silence fell on them all; then Mrs. Treherne heard the kettle boiling over, or said she did, and went into the kitchen.

"You are not eating any breakfast!" said Mary, presently. There was a new note in her voice — half timid, half playful — that brought back the pain to John Harvard's heart, violently.

"No more are you!" he said.

Then they laughed, and being hungry and sensible, ate their breakfast; and then they went out on the verandah and looked about them.

It was a perfect morning. The sea was blue as sapphire; the little harbour was dotted with sails, where the fishermen were starting out for their day's trip; Toluma towered opposite, black against the glowing sky, yet gay here and there with June flowers. Directly below them spread the white beach, and the rocks on either hand, tricked with orange and rose-coloured lichens; while behind, and to right and left, the downs rolled up and away, green and shining, crowned with their sombre woods.

The old house, square and gray and weatherbeaten, stood like a friend beside them. How happy they had been! How could they go away and leave it all?

"Poor old Influence!" said Mary, laying her hand on the mossy door-post. "It has been a happy place for me, surely!"

John Harvard said nothing, only stood aside and looked at her. Her eyes were quite the colour of the sea, he thought, only softer; altogether she was the loveliest thing he had ever seen, but he was not sure that she would care to be told so.

"Come away!" he said, at last. "Let us have one last day that shall be perfection. Let us come to all the places!"

He did not explain what places, but Mary seemed to know, and followed him without a word.

They turned to the left, and took their way over the rocks towards the yew-hollow. The sun shone down into it, waking the warm fragrance into life; little birds flew up from the yew, where they had been breakfasting on the gray-blue berries; a snake, green as emerald, rippled away through the rushes.

"This was the second time I saw you!" said the young man. "The first was just for a minute on the piazza. I say! Do you know, I was awfully put out when I found you were here."

"So was I!" said Mary. "Perfectly furious, when I found you were here!"

"So I inferred!" said John Harvard, dryly. "Then I came up here, that morning, and you were asleep."

"And you were smoking!" said Mary.

"Ah! you woke up, then, when the stone rattled? Well, I wondered how girls of sixteen knew enough to go to college."

"I am twenty!" said Mary, demurely.

"Well, of course, when I found out what a lot you knew—" said John Harvard; "well, anyhow, I wondered— do you mind if I say it? I wondered if you were as pretty awake as you were asleep."

"And was I?" asked Mary, laughing.

"I don't know!" said John Harvard, wickedly. "You wouldn't let me turn round. That was the next time, when—"

"Don't!" cried Mary, blushing scarlet, and springing up from her seat on the yew-bed. "I don't care to recall that time, sir! You took me for a sheep, you may remember."

"I know I was an ass!" said the young man, meekly. "Quite an Animals' Fair between us, don't you think? And then — the next time — for I don't count the times you whisked by me in the house, with your head in the air — the next time was in the Black Woods. That was — quite a time! Shall we go there, — Miss Smith?"

"No, Mr. Harvard, we shall not! And it would be a pity for you to be impertinent on our last day. We will go to Black Head, and to Gull Rock, and to all the dear, dear pools and dikes and precipices. And as we go, — since you are so fond of reminiscences, — I can remind you of the baby and the pin."

"Don't!" cried the youth, in his turn. "I call a truce! and how could I be supposed to know?"

"But you may sing 'Toreador'!" said Mary, with no special relevance.

"There is another song that I like better now!" said John Harvard. "I have been singing it to myself ever since — that is, for some time. May I sing it to you?"

Of course he could, and did.

> "Quand j'ai vu Madeline
> Pour la première fois — "

His voice thrilled deep and sweet on the quiet air, and there was something in it that made Mary's heart beat fast, and made her feel that it was safer for her to look out to sea, or down at the rocks, or anywhere save up at the brown eyes that she knew were bent on her as the lad sang.

Ah! that was a day! Nature seemed to know all about it. The sea laughed and dimpled all over with happy lights. The sun winked and twinkled with merriment. The brown old rocks smiled, and made themselves as soft and comfortable as their nature allowed; the ripples lapped softly in the chasms, the breeze came like a kiss. Ah! that was a day!

And when it was over; when the blazing gold had gathered itself into one splendid glory over the black head of Toluma, and the sea was deepening into purple, and the rosy shades were softening to amethyst and gray and nameless hues of harmony and rest, these two young people sat together on the verandah of the Influence, and watched the lovely pomp, and saw the world that it was very good. They had just come from the early evening service in the chapel, a service so sweet, so earnest and simple, that their hearts were full. The melody of the closing hymn was ringing in their ears, and Mary repeated the words softly:

"God be with you till we meet again!"

"And when will that be?" asked John Harvard, in a low voice, his eyes fixed on the golden west.

"Oh!" said Mary, and her voice tried to be light and cheery; "who can tell? We shall surely meet, for have we not resolved to be friends always? Perhaps it may be here again, our next meeting. I shall come again, whenever it is possible. You know I come of island people. My name—" she laughed. "How silly I have been! But of course you have heard it from Mrs. Treherne. My name is Mary Weymouth. My people came from here. Indeed, I have always liked to think that we are descended from Captain Weymouth of the *Archangel*, the first white man who ever saw this beloved island of ours."

"Oh! if you come to that," said the young man, "my name is John Rosier, and my ancestor came on the *Archangel*, too."

"What!" cried Mary. "James Rosier, gentleman, who wrote the story of the great voyage? Oh, Mr. Harvard, you don't really—no! You are making fun of me. It would be too good to be true."

"Fact, I assure you!" said the young man. "Ask Mrs. Treherne else! Do you mean to say she hasn't told you all this?"

"I — wouldn't let her!" said Mary, in a small voice.

She was silent for a moment; then added:

"And for us to meet here, — how very, very strange! But — of course, this is most delightful and astonishing, and all, — but — I am almost sorry that you are not John Harvard after all!"

"I am John!" said the young man.

They were silent again. Then, under the soft, gray twilight, he put out his hand, and took the girl's hand, and held it in his strong, warm clasp.

"Mary!" he said, and his deep voice trembled a little. "Mary, dear, the old 'Influence' has justified its name, has it not? I — I don't know how it may be with you, but you fill my heart and my life; there is no one else in the world for me. See, dear! Our ancestors — those old beggars — came a long way together, and found this island, the best place in the world, I —"

"Oh, yes!" whispered Mary.

"And — they were rather a set of rascals, I believe, but still it was a great thing they did, and I shall bless them for it as long as I live. Mary, dear, shall we follow where they led the way? Shall we take our voyage together?"

He bent his head over the slender hand. The shadows gathered deeper; the violet dusk came softly over the earth and wrapped her mantle round the lovers.

Presently Mrs. Treherne came to see why her boarders did not heed the tea-bell; but after peeping through the parlour blinds for a moment, she went back again, and sat down in the rocking-chair, and rocked to and fro, and cried with pleasure.

"It shall be called the 'Influence,'" she said; "and the 'Landlady's Delight!'"

THE END.

www.ingramcontent.com/pod-product-compliance
Lightning Source LLC
Chambersburg PA
CBHW031406160426
43196CB00007B/917